04/08

D   ns

T   ERED FRIEND

RD HALL

LONDON TOWN PRESS

Jean-Michel Cousteau *presents*

Jean-Michel Cousteau
Publishing Director

Series Editor
Vicki León

A Charm of Dolphins
Principal photographer
Howard Hall

Additional photographers
Frank Balthis, Jim Brandenberg, David Doubilet, Jeff Foott,
François Gohier, Martha Hill/Kevin Schafer, Helmet Horn,
Stephen Krasemann, Stephen Leatherwood, Philip Rosenberg,
Marty Snyderman, Norbert Wu

London Town Press
P.O. Box 585
Montrose, California 91021
www.LondonTownPress.com

Book design by Christy Hale
10   9   8   7   6   5   4   3   2   1

Printed in Singapore

Distributed by Publishers Group West

Library of Congress Cataloging-in-Publication Data
Hall, Howard
A charm of dolphins : the threatened life of a flippered friend /
by Howard Hall.—2nd ed.
p. cm.—(Jean-Michel Cousteau presents)
Includes bibliographical references and index.
ISBN 978-0-9766134-8-0 (trade paper)
1. Dolphins—Juvenile literature. [1. Dolphins.] I. Title.
QL737.C432H35 2007
599.53—dc22
2007000260

FRONT COVER: A bottlenose dolphin, its dorsal fin visible above the surface, moseys through shallow warm seas. It lives near Belize, home to the longest barrier reef in the western hemisphere.

TITLE PAGE: Dolphins like this bottlenose are built with long jaws and upturned mouths. When they open their mouths, they look like they are smiling. This is one of the reasons dolphins are loved.

BACK COVER: Two spotted dolphin juveniles head for the surface in the waters of the Atlantic Ocean. A very social species, they touch often. They can also play rough; some males even fight for dominance within their group. There are two species of spotted dolphins. They prefer warmer waters, living from the Red Sea to Florida to the Pacific Ocean.

Contents

The friendliest smile in the sea

▶ Atlantic spotted dolphins play a fast game of keep-away, using a bright red scarf. The animals with the most spots are adults. Juveniles take ten years or more to get the markings of an adult.

There I was, twenty feet underwater on the white sands of the Grand Bahamas Bank. I took a breath from my scuba regulator and held it, listening. Yes, I could hear them, an orchestra of whistles and percussion. And if I could hear them, they could "see" me. The tumult grew louder until it surrounded me. Suddenly they were rocketing by from all directions. Dolphins!

"Hello, old friends," I said silently. Already I recognized animals I'd known for years. The one I called Stubby. Another, the female I'd nicknamed Chopper. And Chopper, I saw, had a young calf with her now!

Swirling around me were the Atlantic spotted dolphins I had visited nearly every year for a dozen years.

From my wetsuit I pulled a bright red scarf I'd borrowed from our boat. Holding it in front of me, I began swimming away from the animals, using my swimfins to imitate their dolphin-kick moves. They overtook me in seconds. I tried to turn away, swimming as fast as I could. They anticipated every clumsy move. Within

◄While playing keep-away and other games, dolphins balance objects like a scarf on their beaks, dorsal fins, even their tail flukes. Like our games, dolphin play has rules. The second dolphin can't pick up the scarf until the first one has dropped it.

seconds I was nearly exhausted. I released the scarf, turning just in time to see a young female dolphin catch it on one of her small flippers or pectoral fins.

Resting, I knelt on the bottom and watched as the young female raced around me with the scarf on her fin, a dozen other dolphins in hot pursuit. After a few minutes she let it slip to her tail flukes. She continued to race, the faces of other dolphins just inches from the scarf. Finally she let go. Instantly another dolphin had it on its nose.

There were rules to this keep-away game. You weren't allowed to steal the scarf from another dolphin until it was released. The game was to stay close enough so that you were first to get the scarf when the holder decided to give it up. It was a good game. I'd learned it from the dolphins. Often I'd watched them play it, using strands of seaweed. The red scarf was my contribution.

The dolphins zoomed around, passing the flowing cloth deftly from nose to flipper to dorsal fin to tail with complete

control. After a short break, I rejoined the game to try my luck again.

Since the dolphins seemed to sense when I was holding back, I swam as fast as I could, straining to grab that piece of red cloth. With playful ease, the dolphins kept it inches from my grasp. One dropped it a foot from my fingers. Before I could reach it, another snatched it up. Finally the dolphins gave me a break. As I neared exhaustion and slowed down, the scarf was deposited in front of me. All of them held back just long enough for me to capture it.

For a few seconds I swam in triumph, holding the scarf high. When I dropped it again, another dolphin dove on the red cloth in a flash. That did it for me. Tired and nearly out of air, I swam slowly back to the boat, leaving the dolphins behind.

Five minutes later, as I approached the stern of the boat, Chopper raced up and circled for a few slow turns, smiling her dolphin smile at me. Looking closely into the eyes of that wonderful animal, I tried

▶ The dolphin most often seen in captivity, the brainy bottlenose easily learns complex tricks. In the wild, it hunts in ingenious ways. Sometimes bottlenoses circle a school of fish and drive them onto the shore. Bottlenoses also nab octopuses and crabs from shallow water, and dive deep for squid.

to figure out what went on in that magnificent, enormous brain. A moment later, Chopper took off. She left behind a present for me: the red scarf, floating in the water.

These creatures are like no other animals in this world.

When you look at a dolphin, you sense that it really looks back at you. Few people have the privilege, as I do, of playing with dolphins in their natural element. Yet almost everyone is drawn to dolphins. What is it about these creatures that attracts us?

In many ways, dolphins resemble sharks. They have sleek bodies and wear similar colors. Their pointed dorsal fins look much like sharks' fins in the water. They live in the sea, catching fish with their sharp teeth and making baby dolphins. Sharks patrol the same waters, eating fish and making baby sharks. But few people are attracted to sharks. Nobody wants to hug one. On the other hand, if dolphins could sell hugs, they could become rich! What is it about these creatures?

One reason might be their bright eyes and that dolphin "smile," often seen on films and television programs, and even displayed by captive dolphins. Another might be their record of usefulness, even friendship, toward human beings. We have thousands of years of history together. Around the Mediterranean Sea, dolphins were famous for rescuing humans in distress. The ancient Greeks thought so much of dolphins that they made it a capital crime to kill one.

Dolphins help people in other ways, too. In Brazil, bottlenose dolphins herd fish toward the beach so that local fishermen can net them. Fish that escape the nets swim back to the waiting dolphins. Human records tell us that dolphins have been cooperating to fish like this for 160 years!

▶ Big-eyed dolphins have good eyesight above and below the water. Through their skin and flippers, they feel and touch the objects in their world. Young and old often play touching games. But the most important sense for dolphins is hearing. Using organs in their round foreheads, dolphins echolocate, a super form of sonar.

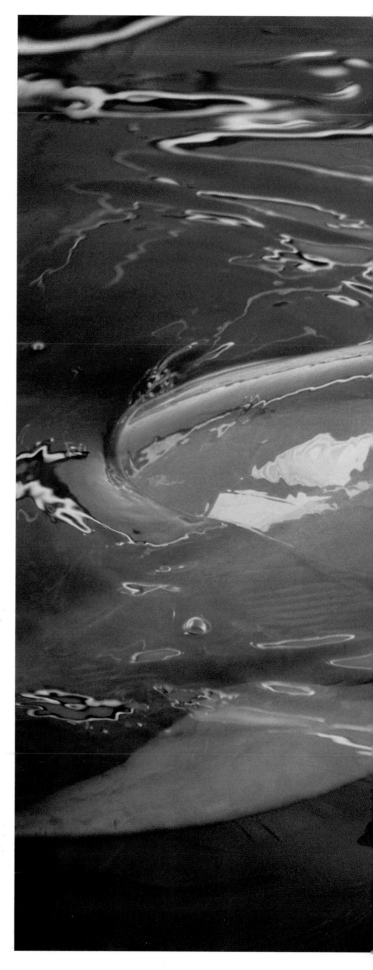

*T*he bodies of dolphins look shark-like but they're more closely related to human beings than to fish. Even though they live in the ocean, dolphins are warm-blooded mammals like us. They breathe air, nurse their young, and have hair. I wouldn't call dolphins hairy; a few bristles on their snouts, and that's it. Still, many mammals, from elephants to armadillos, have very little hair.

Dolphins are small toothed whales belonging to the order Cetacea. Scientists divide cetaceans into two suborders: the Mysticeti or baleen whales, and the Odontoceti or toothed whales.

Baleen whales tend to be huge. Their mouths contain baleen plates full of comb-

◄ Wild dolphins soar into the air for many reasons. Sometimes to spot schools of fish. Other times, to scare schooling fish into a tighter ball. Once in awhile, they jump for the fun of it.

▼ In many ways, a killer whale is an oversized dolphin. Its mouth looks much like a dolphin's mouth but it has only 50 teeth. Its bigger teeth work well, however, to capture prey as large as seals.

◄ Depending on species, a dolphin may have as many as 170 teeth. Their cone-shaped choppers allow them to grab fishy prey or tasty squid, then swallow food whole. Dolphins never chew their food.

like bristles that strain seawater to find the whale's food: almost-invisible plankton and tiny fishes. The baleen suborder includes the gray whale and the blue whale, the largest creature that has ever lived.

Toothed whales like killer whales and dolphins use sharp teeth to catch fish, squid, and other prey. Most of the marine mammals we call "dolphins" belong to the Delphinidae family. The term "porpoise" usually refers to animals in the Phocoenidae family. To marine biologists, all of these animals are simply toothed whales. This group includes 32 species of dolphins and six porpoise species.

More than two-thirds of our world is covered with water. Dolphins have successfully evolved to live in most of these watery habitats: from the Arctic to the Antarctic, in warm water and in cold, in salt water and even in fresh water.

Most species live in the relatively shallow waters around islands and continents. A few live in landlocked seas, like the Baltic and Black Seas. Some make their homes in the vast open ocean. And a few species abandoned salt water altogether to live in rivers.

The great granddaddy ancestor of all whales and dolphins lived on earth more than 50 million years ago. Scientists think it was a land mammal, a 4-legged, dog-sized predator. As millions of years passed, certain descendants of this hairy hunter evolved into the animals we call pigs, camels, and deer.

Other descendants reentered the water, eventually evolving into whales. Why did they go back to the sea? Changes in their environment, perhaps, or increased competition from other animals. For more than 40 million years, dolphins and whales have been sea creatures; they've looked much like modern species for ten million years. Over time, the process of natural selection transformed these meat-eating land mammals into creatures resembling dolphins.

What exactly is natural selection? It's a process of genetic trial and error. It works a bit like this.

Suppose you were born with a nose at the top of your forehead. Sure, you look funny. But if your survival depends on catching fish and you can breathe better through your funny nose while swimming, you'll probably catch more fish; enough food so that you live long enough to raise lots of children. Some of your children will end up with your nose, which won't seem so funny any more.

Through natural selection, nostrils migrated to the tops of dolphin heads. The front limbs of dolphins eventually became flippers or pectoral fins. Tails became flukes. Features common to all mammals got modified to serve a creature living entirely in the sea. Look at a dolphin skeleton, and you'll see the remnants of front limbs in the pectoral fins. They include all of the same bones found in the human hand. You can even find small bones (now serving no purpose) which correspond to the pelvis and hind legs of the dolphin's ancient land ancestor.

In the ocean, animal limbs melt away, ears become internal, and bodies get streamlined for several reasons. One is speed—and the dolphin has it. It's the cheetah of the sea.

Compared to most other fishes and marine mammals, dolphins are lightning fast. In some dolphin species, individuals can hit 25 miles per hour for extended periods. When you're swimming in the thicker medium of water, that is speeding! Most ocean-going ships powered by huge engines chug along at less than 20 miles per hour.

Some sharks can keep up with a fast-moving dolphin—but only for a few minutes. Sharks don't get enough oxygen passing through their gills to permit marathon speed-swimming. Once the energy stored in a shark's muscles is used up, it must slow down to rest or exhaust itself in a minute or two.

Dolphins don't bother with the small amounts of oxygen dissolved in water. They breathe air, which is 21 percent oxygen, compared to sea water, which is less than one percent oxygen. This amount of oxygen allows dolphins to power along at high speeds for many minutes.

These animals are no slouches at diving, either. Bottlenose dolphins often dive to 500 feet and have gone as deep as 1,000

▶ Three bottlenose dolphins go head to head. These marine mammals vocalize constantly, making clicks and squeaks. In addition, special communication takes place with the help of those melon-shaped foreheads. They use an animal sonar called echolocation.

▲ Dolphins have an efficient way to travel fast, called porpoising. They swim underwater, using their tails for power to jump in a forward motion in the air. While airborne, they take a new breath before diving again.

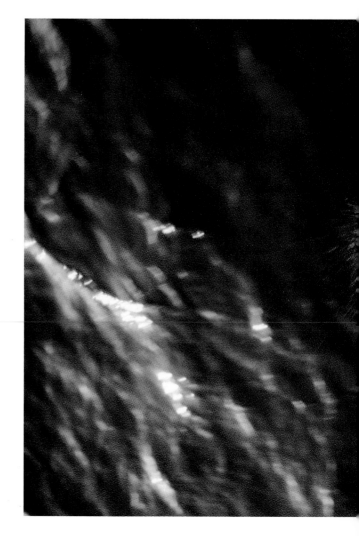

feet. On average, they can stay ten minutes underwater.

A dolphin often uses a special method to swim fast, called porpoising. The animal starts underwater by beating its tail flukes hard, then propels itself into the air where it takes a breath before sliding neatly back into the sea. Porpoising is an energy-efficient way to travel at high speed. These jumps send the animal high into the air and also in a forward direction, as much as three times its body length.

At other times, dolphins follow boats to bow-ride, swimming in the pressure wave formed by a ship's movement. This provides

▼ Even though dolphins are fast and tireless swimmers, they do enjoy hitching rides. They often ride the pressure wave or slipstream formed by a ship's bow moving through the water. They also catch the pressure waves made by larger whales, such as the gray.

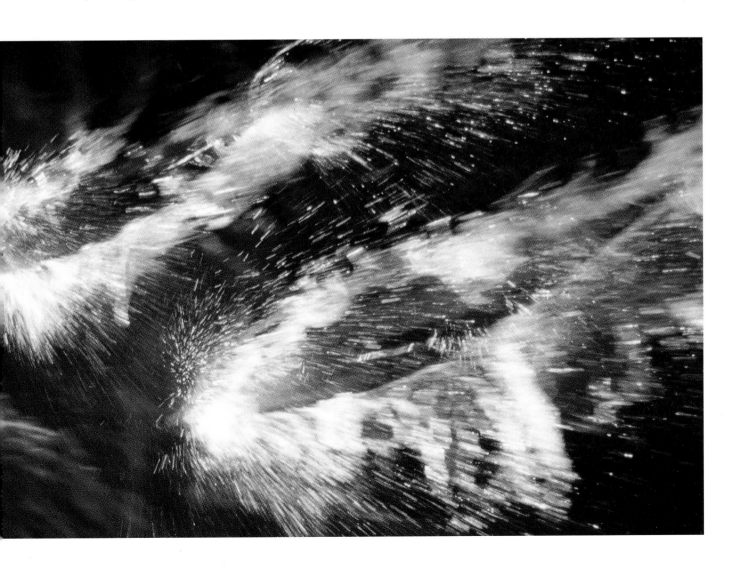

▲ Dolphins cannot dive as deeply as the bigger whales or elephant seals do. Still they go deeper than human beings can, from 500 to 1,000 feet. Some species are able to stay underwater for up to ten minutes.

more speed with less effort. Dolphins follow behind larger whales for the same reason.

During my years in the ocean, I've often had good reason to notice the resemblance between dolphins and sharks. Sometimes I've been startled underwater by a distant dark silhouette that appears to be a large shark. Then the shark-like silhouette moves, and I realize I've been looking at a dolphin.

Although their shapes and fins are very similar, dolphins and sharks move differently. Sharks and other fishes move their tails from side to side as they swim. Dolphins swim by moving their tail flukes up and down. This up-and-down movement also helps me tell dolphins from sharks above water.

◄Unlike dolphins, sharks move their tails side to side, like other fishes.

When I spot a shark fin on the surface, it usually moves straight ahead. A dolphin fin on the surface rises and falls as the animal swims.

Kids often ask, "What's it like to hug a dolphin?" To me, the smooth thick skin of a dolphin has a rubbery feel, like an inflated inner-tube. Bottlenose dolphins, often seen in coastal areas and in captivity, have shiny gray skin. Other species may have skin that's black and white, spotted or striped. These animals have no arms or fingers but their skin is very sensitive. Juveniles and adults often play touch games. Dolphins may greet each other by rubbing flippers.

▼ As a bottlenose swims over a shallow reef, it moves its powerful tail in an up-and-down motion, like whales do.

▲ Bottlenose dolphins in captivity make perfect leaps together over their trainer's head. It's easy to see that bottlenoses and other dolphin species weigh much more than humans and can be up to twice as long.

Face to face, dolphins are bigger than you imagine. They weigh over 600 pounds and can be up to ten feet long. Even the harbor porpoise, one of the smallest species, gets six feet long and may weigh up to 100 pounds.

The most distinctive feature of a dolphin is its head. On top is a hole that looks like a big belly-button. Called the blowhole, it's the dolphin version of a nose. Expressive eyes lie below the blowhole on either side of the head. The sleek round forehead, called a "melon," holds a big brain, fatty tissue, and organs the dolphin uses to explore its world and communicate.

Some species, like the spotted dolphin, the spinner, and the bottlenose, have long tapered beaks or snouts. Other species, like the dusky and Risso's dolphins, have shorter beaks—or none at all.

Being meat-eaters, dolphins have long jaws that hold up to 170 cone-shaped teeth. Depending on species, they consume squid, clams, crab, shrimp, and a wide variety of fish.

Finally, these graceful animals possess tapering dorsal and pectoral fins plus a muscular tail. The two-fluked tail, similar to the tails on larger whales, power the animal, allowing it to make those spectacular leaps, spins, and dolphin acrobatics.

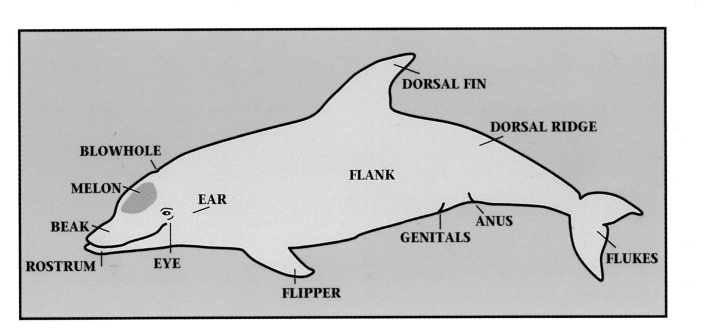

Familiar yet still mysterious

▶How many ways can a dolphin leap? Too many to count. Several species, including spinner and common dolphins, frolic in the warm waters of Baja California. Some of them spin like tops as they jump.

Some people have seen wild dolphins soaring and spinning above the waves. Many more have enjoyed their jumping at marine parks or in films. Certain species can soar 20 feet above the surface—higher than a two-story house! At marine parks, they jump because the trainers "pay" them with fish. But why do they jump in the wild?

On calm days in Mexico's Sea of Cortez, I've been lucky enough to see up to a thousand dolphins at a time. These groups, sometimes called pods or schools, stretch from horizon to horizon. In them, dozens of dolphins leap high into the air at one time. It's a dazzling sight. Seeing them, it seems certain that they jump for pure joy, and that nothing could be more fun than to be a dolphin. Even though I'm trained as a biologist, I feel sure that dolphins do lots of things simply for the fun of it.

There may be practical reasons for their aerial displays too. High leaps let them

◀It's a thrilling sight, watching dolphins leap, jump, and make other acrobatic displays in the air. These common dolphins in Mexico's Sea of Cortez often swim and soar together in large groups. As many as one thousand animals have been seen at a time.

◄ Four kinds or subspecies of spinner dolphins can be found in the Pacific, Atlantic, and Indian oceans. Spinners may weigh as much as 160 pounds. A lot of that weight is muscle, allowing them to jump very high and spin two or three times in the air before they splash down.

search the ocean surface for schools of fish. Dolphins often work together to herd fishes and disorient them for feeding purposes. Dusky dolphins are known to do this. Their jumps may also frighten fishy prey and keep them close together. Jumping would show where seabirds are feeding, a sure sign of schooling fish nearby.

It's also possible that dolphins jump to shake off parasites. Or to communicate with each other. Or even for reasons we haven't figured out yet.

Various species of dolphins make other surface displays. They breach, exploding out of the water to fall back with a big splash. They make noise by lobtailing—smacking their tail flukes—on the surface. Spinner and striped dolphins do aerial somersaults or appear to "stand" on top of the water and spin in circles on their tails.

Like orcas, their close kin, dolphins are social animals. Some species live and move in big groups. Others live in small family pods with mother and calf pairs as the basic unit. Dolphins often swim, dive, and hunt side by side, in pairs or in larger groups. This behavior begins very early.

Atlantic spotted dolphins travel in tight groups. When they are about three years old and no longer in their mother's care, male juveniles peel off to form their own "gang."

Risso's dolphin, the biggest species, frequents the Azores in the north Atlantic. It may associate with as few as three individuals or in super-pods of several thousand animals.

Although mating and birth have been observed among captive dolphins, we still know little about reproduction in the wild. We do know that the males of some species fight over females. Courting and mating appear to be brief, belly to belly encounters. Afterward, the female is on her own.

Most species seem to give birth to one calf per year. A baby dolphin enters the world well developed and ready to swim. Some dolphin newborns are one-third the size of their mothers. That would be like a human mother giving birth to a five-year-old! Dolphin babies emerge tail-first. Adult females sometimes help with the birth, pushing the newborn upward for its first breath. Swimming means survival, since the baby emerges from its mother's warmth into often frigid water where it must quickly surface to breathe air or drown.

▲ Like its mother and father, a baby dolphin breathes air. At birth, it comes out tail-first. Right away it needs to reach the surface of the water. Sometimes other female dolphins help the mother and the newborn, pushing it upward for its first breath.

▲ Dolphin mothers and calves stay close for one to three years, male calves for even longer. The calf nurses often and drinks milk even after its teeth come in. Its mother teaches it to hunt and to socialize with the group. Dolphin fathers don't seem to play any part in rearing the young.

Nursing often on rich milk, the young dolphin stays close to its mother until weaned. It glides easily in the slipstream produced by its mother as she swims. The mother-calf relationship may last one to three years, perhaps longer in some dolphin species.

The mother teaches her young how to catch prey. Recently I watched bottlenose dolphins at work. Ten of them were hunting reef fish in the Bahamas. The adults swam to the bottom, chasing fishes into narrow cracks and crevices—then blasted the fish with high-intensity sound. As the fishes came flying out, the young dolphins chased them. If a youngster didn't catch prey before it found a new place to hide, the adult scared it out again.

It was amazing and amusing. Sometimes six adults at a time had their beaks close to the rocky reef where the fishes were. Meanwhile, the still-clumsy baby dolphins chased the fish, mostly without success.

These sound blasts were fairly intense, as though they were trying to stun the fish as well as frighten them. The fishes that escaped seemed undamaged, however. A few minutes later, I heard an unfamiliar sound. Besides the typical dolphin clicks and whistles, I heard loud bangs that sounded like pistols being fired underwater. This stronger sound: was it a new way to stun prey?

Dolphins do more than teach their young to fish. Scientists in western Australia have observed tool use among bottlenose dolphins in Shark Bay. Females break off sponges from the seabed, wearing them on their beaks as they hunt. The sponge seems to help them uncover hidden fishes—and it protects beaks from the stings of poisonous stonefish. By studying the dolphins' DNA, scientists also found that dolphin mothers mainly teach this sponging behavior to female offspring.

Although we use our hearing a great deal, we relate to the outside world primarily through sight. For dolphins, however, vision isn't nearly as important as hearing.

Dolphins (along with many whale species) understand their world mainly through sound. This makes sense. Sound travels five times faster through water than through air. In addition, seawater is often dark and murky. Light has difficulty traveling through it.

They use sound in several ways, the most important being echolocation. To locate objects and find prey, a dolphin makes sounds inside its head, projecting them through an oil-filled sac in its forehead. Like a radar gun, the animal shoots sound waves of clicks in the direction it wants to "see." As the echoes bounce off the fish and return, the dolphin is sending out more clicks. The time between each click and its echo tells the dolphin how far away the object is.

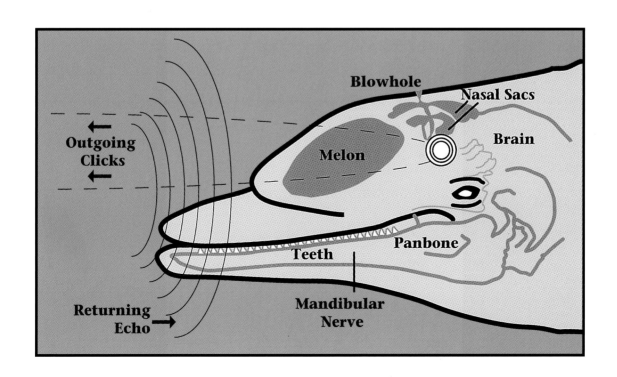

These reflected sound waves are turned into a "audio picture" of its environment by the dolphin's busy brain. It can track several targets at different distances at the same time. Some researchers believe that echolocation even lets one dolphin tell what kind of mood another is in.

These capabilities seem like super-powers. In one study, a dolphin was blindfolded, then offered two fishes—one real and the other accurate but artificial—and had no trouble telling the difference. The animal was able to do this even at a distance. Echolocation may even allow dolphins to "look" inside a live fish to see its density and internal structures, a bit like x-ray vision.

Another study with captive dolphins showed that an individual didn't have to see an item, or echolocate at it, to identify it. Instead, it simply listened to another dolphin's click signals as it was presented with the same item.

New research done on rough-toothed dolphins in the wild seems to confirm that theory. When these dolphins swam apart from one another, scattered across the water, they produced various echolocation signals. But when they swam close together in synchronized formations, the biologist tracking them found that only one animal

produced clicks. Can dolphins "tune in" to each other's echolocation and use the information? Thomas Gotz, a German scientist, thinks so. Others like New Zealand researcher Steve Dawson agree. He believes that the dolphin ability to "eavesdrop" on each other may have co-evolved with their cooperative behavior.

I often try to imagine what seeing with sound is like. When diving with dolphins, I get a thorough inspection by the animals. As they approach, I hear a variety of whistles and clicks. As they get closer, the clicks get louder and faster until they sound like a zipper being unzipped. The sound pulses bounce around in the air cavity of my lungs. It feels very strange. I wish I could ask the dolphins if my appendix looks okay, or if there is any sign of plaque buildup in my arteries.

Compared with animals of similar size, dolphins have huge brains—equal or greater in size and complexity than human ones.

What do they do with that brainpower? Nobody really knows. But they are certainly

◄ Swimming with dolphins to photograph them is a diver's dream. The animals seem more comfortable around human beings without scuba gear, like this diver-photographer. Perhaps the sound of bubbles in the water from the scuba gear disturbs them.

▲ Many species prefer coastal waters close to the shore, like these bottlenose dolphins swimming past waterfalls in New Zealand. There are nearly 40 species of dolphins and porpoises. They live in almost all of the watery habitats on our planet.

doing something with it. Brains are very energy-expensive organs. The old saying, "use it or lose it," holds true when it comes to body parts and evolution.

So dolphins must need brains that require size and complexity. It's difficult for human researchers to conduct intelligence studies in wild dolphin populations. But sometimes the things learned about captive dolphins prove to be insightful about wild populations too. One study found that dolphins recognize themselves in mirrors. Before this, scientists had thought that self-awareness was only possible in animals with frontal lobes— meaning human beings and primates. Now we have more proof that dolphins have a very clear sense of themselves and others.

Do dolphins have language? Probably not by our definition. Do they communicate? Yes, indeed. Many of the sounds produced by dolphins aren't used for echolocation but carry information.

For instance, early in life each dolphin gives itself a "name," a signature whistle unique to itself. Members of its social group recognize each other by their whistle names, not merely by the sound of a familiar dolphin voice.

Dolphins spend most of their time in the company of other dolphins, sometimes in groups, other times with relatives or a particular individual. In ocean waters, often pitch-black or cloudy, signature whistles make it easier for dolphins to find one another. Species that spend their lives in large groups with lots of interaction, like the bottlenose, must find whistle names very useful.

I think questions about dolphin intelligence, memory, language, and communication are among the world's greatest mysteries. They are questions about reality itself. The dolphin brain works in a world much different than our own. Perhaps in the future, technology or evolution will allow us to share the dolphin's reality. If so, it will be one of humanity's greatest adventures.

▶ Dolphins often swim together in groups called pods or schools. Their ability to echolocate, a form of sonar, keeps them from bumping into each other at night and in inky-black waters.

Porpoise to boto & beyond

▶ Off California's shores, Pacific white-sided dolphins hunt underwater for schooling fish and squid. This short-beaked species moves in groups of ten to 100—sometimes more. It often rides in the wake of boats. At other times, this acrobat shows off in mid-air, doing spectacular somersaults.

I'm often asked: what's the difference between dolphins and porpoises? The words "dolphin" and "porpoise" are not scientific terms. To marine biologists, all of these animals are simply toothed whales, with most dolphin species being classified with the Delphinidae family and most porpoises with the Phocoenidae family.

Six species of porpoise inhabit the watery parts of our world, from the black-and-white Dall's porpoise of the northern Pacific to the dainty vaquita native to Mexico's Sea of Cortez, smallest of all the cetaceans.

The word "porpoise" comes from the Latin words for "pig" and "fish." Some species make a sneezy grunt as they surface—perhaps that's why they got stuck with the pig label. These often chubby animals have blunt heads that lack the slim dolphin beaks. Most are shy underwater mammals, seldom making spectacular jumps

◄ The pinkish-gray boto, one of five species of fresh-water dolphins, has tiny eyes and poor vision. Instead, it relies on echolocation and its long snout to nose out fishes and invertebrates on the river bottom. The muddy brown waters of the Amazon and Orinoco Rivers of South America are the boto's home.

▲ Spotted dolphins don't wear a full coat of spots until they get to be of breeding age. These Atlantic spotted dolphins must be eleven years old or more.

or displays. Some porpoise populations are shrinking fast because they live in shallow waters and estuaries—the same places where human development, boat traffic, and pollution are highest.

The strangest members of the dolphin clan are the fresh-water dolphins. They include the susu, a stocky fellow with a skinny beak and Mr. Magoo eyesight that navigates the Ganges and other rivers in India by echolocation. In the rainforest, the boto is quite at home in the milk-chocolate waters of the Amazon river, using its long snout to nose out crab and fishes. When local rivers flood, the boto swims among rainforest trees to hunt.

The most familiar species include the common dolphin, found all over the world. A mid-sized animal, its yellow patches and hourglass markings make it

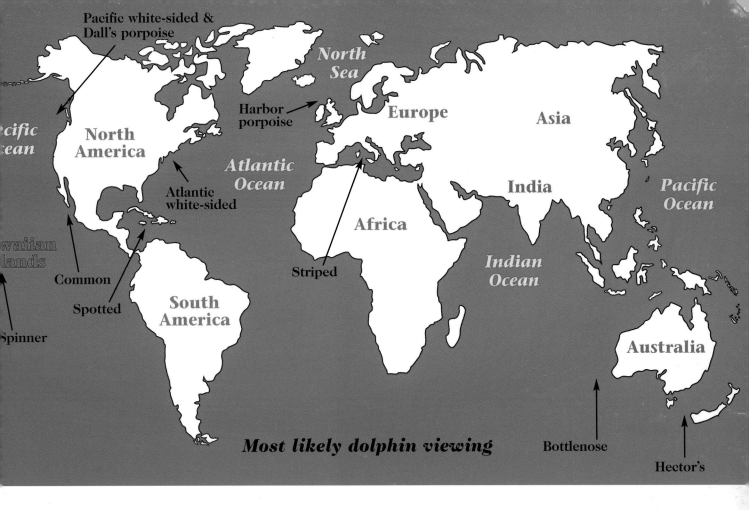

Pacific white-sided &
Dall's porpoise

North
Sea

Europe

Asia

Harbor
porpoise

*Pacific
Ocean*

North
America

*Atlantic
Ocean*

India

*Pacific
Ocean*

Atlantic
white-sided

Africa

*Indian
Ocean*

Striped

Common

Hawaiian
Islands

Spotted

South
America

Australia

Spinner

Most likely dolphin viewing

Bottlenose

Hector's

▲ Dolphins roam widely, but you are most likely to spot these dolphin species in the areas marked.

---

easy to identify. The sight of hundreds of them hop-scotching across turquoise waters is unforgettable.

Spotted dolphins swim fast, play hard, and breach high. There are two species; both cruise warmer waters and their populations overlap in the Atlantic, especially around the Bahamas.

The animal beloved by the ancient Greeks is the striped dolphin, with markings so beautiful it looks like a painting. Traveling in groups of 25 or more, it

preys on anchovies and squid and is found throughout a wide band of ocean waters around the world, not just the Mediterranean.

The most famous and beloved dolphin is probably the bottlenose, thanks to its appearance as "Flipper" and on countless television programs and films. It's also the dolphin most often seen in captivity. Although it has a friendly screen image, the bottlenose can be aggressive toward other dolphins and whales. In the wild, it lives in a complex society, divided into all-male and all-female groups. Males sometimes fight each other for access to females. In contrast, female bottlenoses sometimes band together to fight off sharks that attack their young. They're not afraid to head-butt a six-foot-long shark!

Whether we'll ever be able to communicate with dolphins in the future depends on whether they survive the mass extinctions of species on our planet. Tens of thousands of animal species have disappeared during the age of mankind. Many whale species are gravely threatened, including the dolphins. As intelligent as we take credit for being, we haven't been very smart when it comes to taking care of our land and water home.

Our mistreatment of the oceans has affected dolphins in several critical ways. Seawater pollution levels are rising sharply. In some places, dead dolphins are washing ashore because the ocean has literally

▲ Dolphins may live ten to 50 years in the wild. Far too often, however, their lives are cut short by human actions. Huge fishing nets like this one cause a cruel death for hundreds of thousands of dolphins each year.

become too toxic for them to live in. The dumping of sewage, pesticide runoff, chemicals, and industrial wastes has weakened dolphin populations, making them more susceptible to diseases and parasites. Pollution may also affect reproductive rates among dolphin species.

The most severe threat, however, is 21st-century commercial fishing. Starting in the 1950s, fishing as a way of life quickly grew into a huge, international industry. The main reason? The invention of strong nylon mesh, which made it possible to fish with huge nets. In 40 years, an estimated six million dolphins were killed—not for their meat, but as by-catch or incidental kill in these massive nets, some of them 25 miles long. As nets this size are pulled in, countless dolphins get trapped and killed in the process.

Many of those millions of dead dolphins lost their lives in purse-seine nets used for tuna fishing. In the waters of the eastern Pacific, however, spinner dolphins weren't caught by accident. They were deliberately hunted. Why? Because tuna fishermen knew that schools of yellowtail tuna would be found beneath the spinner dolphins.

Whether the nets used are gillnets, purse seine, or driftnets, they often strip-mine the sea, catching whales, sea turtles, and birds as well as dolphins and the targeted fish, such as tuna or squid. Their use has pushed some dolphin species, from Mexico's vaquita to New Zealand's Maui dolphin, to the razor edge of extinction.

Public outrage and the threat of boycotts in the 1990s caused three major U.S. canneries to stop buying tuna caught in this fashion and ensure their tuna was "dolphin safe." European canneries followed their lead. Sad to say, however, other countries still continue to fish for tuna that is captured at the expense of thousands of dolphins. And other canneries continue to buy tuna that costs dolphins their lives.

Overfishing worldwide now presents the scariest threat to dolphins and many marine animals. Overfishing has left many fishermen with no fish to catch. In some places, they've turned to dolphins, selling their meat to protein-hungry markets in an overpopulated world.

In addition, dolphins are now forced to compete with human beings for the sea's

◄ Most human beings care about dolphins. Caring trainers often bond with dolphins, making their lives in captivity better. But wild dolphin populations are threatened. Big fisheries continue to waste the lives of these highly intelligent creatures, killing them in the hunt for tuna and other commercial species of fish.

▶ Nowadays dolphins are forced to compete with human beings over the shrinking world supply of fish. Sometimes they are wrongly blamed for catching fish the fishermen want. In this 1980 massacre at Iki Island, Japanese fishermen corralled dolphins in a bay, then speared hundreds to death. The slaughter drew public outrage and led to some reforms. Still the senseless killing of dolphins, especially through the use of giant nets, continues.

resources. At Iki Island, one of Japan's few remaining fishing grounds, fishermen believe that dolphins hunt tuna, the same prey they want. Instead of blaming over-fishing, the real cause, frustrated fishermen trap the dolphins in the bay and kill them with spears. In 1980, I was an eyewitness to this bloody, gut-wrenching experience. The hundreds of dolphins I saw massacred ended up as fertilizer!

Iki Island is just one example of traditional fishing cultures around the globe that compete with dolphins over food in an ocean of shrinking resources. If dolphins lose this contest, they often pay with their lives.

As individuals, most human beings are fond of dolphins. As a species, however, we are wiping out entire populations of these wonderful creatures. What can you and I do to end this terrible waste of intelligent life?

Get educated about the issues that affect the ocean's health. Make sure everyone

in your family, does, too. Join some of the worthy advocacy groups and environmental organizations that push for reforms to clean up our oceans, prevent dumping, and ban driftnets and other non-sustainable methods of fishing. Learn first-hand from scientists what dolphins need by participating in one of the many field programs like Earthwatch.

When buying canned tuna or fresh seafood, ask questions.

Be sure what you eat is dolphin safe. Get a free copy of the Seafood Watch guidelines; they show best choices and fish species to be avoided. Consumer demand keeps fisheries alive—you and your family are consumers. You're entitled to demand alternatives that keep dolphins safe.

Over 500 dolphins live in captivity around the world, most of them to perform and entertain, others used as "therapists"

Atlantic spotted dolphins can move twice as fast as most boats and ships. Sometimes they hit 25 miles an hour. They often travel in small groups or pods. Four of these dolphins are juveniles, with few markings on their sleek skins.

by people seeking relief from medical and mental problems. How can we justify their continued confinement? By promising to give wild dolphins the respect and protection they deserve. And learning to leave the kingdom of dolphins alone. Along with other creatures, they need the freedom to live their wild lives.

The natural world is giving us warning signs, like global warming and species depletion. And more people worldwide, from kids to grownups, are paying attention and trying to turn things around. Perhaps we'll be smart enough to save our planet for ourselves, for dolphins, and for all the creatures that call this planet home. By learning how to become part of the balance of life on earth, only then will we live up to our own definition of intelligence. And human compassion.

Moving like a practiced pair of dancers on the surface of a golden ocean, wild dolphins leap and glide through the swells.

Secrets of dolphins

- What do dolphins drink when they get thirsty? Herring and squid. These and other juicy food favorites contain over 80 percent water.

- Noisy human activities, such as boat motors and underwater explosions, can hurt dolphins. More than sight, they depend on sound and the use of their own "sonar" to hunt and communicate.

▼ Wild dolphins are trusting and helpful animals even though human beings have done them much harm. They often allow divers to get near them. Sometimes they save people from drowning. In a few places where natives still fish in traditional ways, dolphins help by driving fishy prey into the nets. Later they get "paid" with the fishes that escape the nets.

- Why do dolphins live in social groups? To hunt together, swim together, and play together. In a group, a dolphin mother can more easily find a "babysitter" for her new calf, too.

- In some dolphin species, juvenile and adult males hang out together in gangs, showing off to each other with spectacular jumps and acrobatics.

- Bottlenose dolphins give themselves names. To our ears, their names sound like complicated whistles. The animals use these whistle names to find each other in the dark, often murky ocean.

- Some mother dolphins in Australia teach their young to hunt fish with a sponge "tool." The dolphins wear it over their beaks to protect themselves from the stinging stonefish.

- How smart are dolphins? They communicate well, have good memories, and can improvise. As scientists have learned through experiments, dolphins also have self-awareness and can recognize themselves in a mirror.

- Female bottlenose dolphins are fearless mothers. Sometimes they band together to fight off hungry sharks that hunt down their young. Dolphin mothers will even head-butt a shark!

▶ Dolphins of many species feed on squid. In spring, squid rise from deep seas to meet and mate in the sandy clearings near the kelp forest. They provide an all-day, all-night feast for dolphins and other animals.

Glossary

Blowhole. The nostril or opening on top of the dolphin's head connecting to its lungs. It allows the dolphin to expel stale air and inhale fresh air at the surface. Close relatives like gray whales have two blowholes.

Cetacean. All marine mammals that belong to the order Cetacea, commonly referred to as whales. The order is divided into two subgroups, baleen whales and toothed whales, including dolphins.

Dorsal fin. The prominent fin on the back of most dolphin species. Although it may look like the dorsal fin of a shark, the dolphin's fin moves up and down as it travels through the water.

DNA. Short name for the key molecule called deoxyribonucleic acid. Sometimes called the "building block of life," DNA passes along the genetic information of all living things. Marine biologists have used dolphin DNA to learn that female dolphins mainly teach certain behaviors to their female offspring, but not their male offspring.

Echolocation. Animal sonar, a specialized way of hearing underwater, used by dolphins and many whale species. The animal sends out clicking sound waves that echo off the prey fish or object. Quickly the dolphin's brain converts these echoes into a detailed "audio picture." Dolphins can even "read" each other's sonar messages.

Flukes. The powerful tails of dolphins and whales have two flat lobes or flukes, equal in size.

Incidental kill. Also called by-catch, this term refers to marine animals killed through a wasteful practice of fishing for tuna and squid carried out by a few nations and fisheries. They use huge gillnets, driftnets, and purse-seine nets, made of nylon mesh and many miles long. Whether anchored in one place or dragged along the bottom, these nets catch everything, not just target fish. Dead dolphins and other creatures are thrown back in the sea by the thousands.

Melon. The rounded forehead of the dolphin containing its large brain, fatty tissue to protect it, and organs that the animal uses to focus sound for echolocation.

Parasite. An animal that lives on or in its host, sometimes harming it. Dolphins can be troubled by them. Biologists think that they sometimes jump into the air to get rid of parasites.

Pectoral fins. Sometimes called flippers, these fins extend from the chest of the dolphin, helping it move, steer, and explore.

Pod. The name most often used to describe a family or social group of dolphins that move, hunt, and play together. Sometimes these groups are called schools also.

Porpoising. A speedy, energy-efficient method of shallow dives and low jumps that the dolphin uses to travel. As the animal soars above the surface, it takes in air before sliding back into the ocean.

Prey stunning. One of the hunting strategies used by dolphin groups. The animals appear to send out pulses of sound so strong that they stun the fishes being hunted.

Slipstream. The pattern of water turbulence made as a ship or large object moves through it. Also called pressure waves, these slipstreams let dolphins "hitchhike" rides near boats or large whales.

About the author & photographers

During his career, Howard Hall has become one of the world's most respected underwater filmmakers and animal behavioralists. He's received six Emmys, a Golden Panda, and numerous other honors for his "blue chip" natural history films.

As photographer and producer, he has taken part in many films on dolphins, as well as documentaries on whales, sharks, and other marine topics.

Ably assisted by his wife Michele, an underwater photographer and award-winning film producer herself, Howard has created a spectacular series of films in IMAX® format, including his most recent, "Deep Sea 3D".

The Halls have written and photographed other pictorial books, including *A Frenzy of Sharks* and *The Secrets of Kelp Forests* for the Jean-Michel Cousteau Presents series.

Based on their experiences working with dolphins, Howard and Michele have become staunch advocates for the protection of these amazing creatures, whose future wellbeing in the wild is deeply threatened.

As principal photographer, Howard took 15 of the photos in this book, including the front and back covers and pages 4-5, 12, 13, 18 (bottom), 19, 28, 32-33, 34 (bottom), 36, 38-39, 40-41, 45, 46-47. Thirteen other wildlife photographers contributed their artistry to the book: Frank Balthis, pp 16-17, 22; Jim Brandenberg/DRK Photo, p. 29; David Doubilet, p. 15; Jeff Foott, pp 1, 8-9; Francois Gohier, pp 10-11, 18 (top), 23, 42-43; Martha Hill/Kevin Schafer, p. 31; Helmut Horn, pp 20, 37; Stephen Krasemann/DRK Photo, pp 7, 16; Stephen Leatherwood, p. 25; Philip Rosenberg, pp 24, 26; Marty Snyderman, pp 6, 44; Norbert Wu, p. 34 (top).

Special thanks

- Diana Barnhart, Education and Marine Science Advisor
- Dr. Richard Murphy of the Ocean Futures Society

Where to see dolphins

In the wild: It's natural to want to see dolphins up close, to swim with them and photograph them, but human interference can disturb their daily life. Dolphins are legally protected in the U.S. by the Marine Mammal Protection Act, and in other countries as well. For your protection (wild dolphins sometimes bite people when harassed or fearful) and theirs (feeding wild dolphins motivates them to expect handouts and cripples their ability to forage), please do not feed, swim with, or harass wild dolphins. There are gentler ways to experience them. They include volunteering for research expeditions, available through the Earthwatch Institute and other non-profit groups. And sightseeing trips that minimize impact on the animals, such as those run by the Whale and Dolphin Conservation Society.

In captivity: Some marine parks and aquaria no longer display dolphins or have dolphin shows. They can still be seen, however, at the SeaWorlds in California, Texas, and Florida and at certain aquaria around the world, including Shedd Aquarium in Chicago and the Baltimore Aquarium in Maryland.

Helping organizations & good websites

- Whale and Dolphin Conservation Society, Wildlife Centre, Moray Firth, Scotland. A global voice for the protection of dolphins and whales, the WDCS fields a variety of research programs. Its info downloads on dolphin captivity and other topics are very valuable. (www.wdcs.org)
- Earthwatch Institute, 2 Clock Tower Place, #100, Maynard MA 01754. This global organization gets results and helps heal the planet by linking teams of volunteers with scientists and numerous research projects on dolphins and their habitats. Of special interest: hands-on science for the whole family; several teams that include kids 10 and up; teen teams ages 16-17 on dolphins, rainforests, and more. Competitive grants for teachers, free lesson plans from expeditioners too. (www.earthwatch.org)
- National Marine Sanctuary programs. This complex website links to each of the 14 sanctuaries, with lots of goodies at each. Excellent downloads on responsible marine wildlife viewing, the protect dolphin campaign, and more. (www.sanctuaries.noaa.gov)
- The Halls' own website combines stirring photos and amazing video clips with fun stories of their underwater adventures. (www.howardhall.com)
- National Geographic. Frequent updates and breaking news on dolphins and cetaceans at this entertaining and worthy website. (www.nationalgeographic.com)
- Saratoga Dolphin Research Program. The longest-running program of its kind in the world, the SDRP is a regular participant in Earthwatch expeditions. (www.saratogadolphin.org)

To learn more

Books

- *Whalewatcher*, by Trevor Day. (Firefly Books 2006). Invaluable and sensitive reference work, generously illustrated with diagrams, maps, and over 100 photos.
- *Dolphins*, by Michael Bright. (DK Publishing/BBC 2001). For older readers: solid text, behavioral photos and useful diagrams make up this compact 100-page book.
- *California Marine Life*, by Marty Snyderman. (Roberts Rinehart Publishing 1998). A grand field guide, still useful for dolphins and other cetaceans.
- *Secrets of the Ocean Realm*, by Michele & Howard Hall. (Carroll & Graf/Beyond Words 1997). Companion book to a television series filmed and produced by the Halls; lots of exciting behavioral photos and stories, including dolphins.
- *The Secrets of Kelp Forests* and *A Frenzy of Sharks*, by Howard Hall. Newly republished in the Jean Michel Cousteau Presents series.

Videos & DVDs

- "Dolphins, the Wild Side." National Geographic 1999. VHS format, 1 hour. Excellent footage, from hunting sequences to eye-popping dolphin acrobatics.
- "Dolphins." Freeman Films/National Wildlife Federation 2000. IMAX format, 89 minutes. Right-at-you photography, beautiful sequences of many dolphin species, fascinating interviews with scientists and researchers.

▼ Seven spinner dolphins, all in a row, show how this species can jump in and out of the water with such graceful ease.

Index

Photographs are numbered in **boldface** and follow the print references after **PP** (photo page).